Foundation Curriculum
Copyright © 2014
Written by Linda D. Washington
Illustrated by Rebeca Flott
Edited by Joyce S. Pace and Rita K. Jeffries

STORY BOOK LESSON 4
"FORGIVE"

Jesus told us to pray and say,
"Forgive our sins,
just as we forgive everyone who has done wrong to us."

When you asked heavenly Father, He forgave your sins because of Jesus. Let's find out why Jesus wants you to pray and forgive others like Father forgave you!

When you were born again as a child of God, all things in your spirit became new. So now you must learn how to do things new, like your Father and Jesus, in the Kingdom of God.

When Jesus was on earth, the super power of Holy Spirit helped him do everything Father told him. If you received Holy Spirit, you have the same power that Jesus had on earth! Do you know what that means?

It means that the power of Holy Spirit will help you like He helped Jesus! Let's learn about this super power of Holy Spirit in you and how to show others God's Kingdom by the things you choose to do.

The power inside of you is a spirit power. Jesus wants you to know that the things you fight against on earth are spirit things, and he has already beaten them all for you.

Holy Spirit will be with you forever and tell you the truth so you won't be tricked like Adam and Eve. But like Adam and Eve, you must choose who you will obey. Do you remember who Adam and Eve listened to and obeyed?

They listened and obeyed the devil. Did the devil tell the truth or a lie to get Eve to believe him?

The devil always tells lies!
And the devil is still on the earth trying to get everyone to listen and obey him.

The people that killed the body of Jesus also listened and obeyed the devil. But when the spirit of Jesus left His body, the super power of God's Holy Spirit helped Jesus to beat up the devil and all his demons! They are so afraid of Jesus that the demons tremble, shake, and run away fast whenever someone like you says the name of Jesus!

Let's clap and cheer for Jesus,
"YAAAY Jesus!

We are clapping and cheering for you!
You are our Super Hero!"

Jesus wants you to know and remember that the super power of God in you which is the Holy Spirit, is BIGGER and GREATER, than ALL the power of the devil! You do not have to be afraid of any evil thing.

Father was so happy Jesus believed and obeyed Him that He made Jesus the King over all kings! And guess what Jesus did?

Jesus made everyone who believes him a king too! So if you said that you believe Jesus, you are a king! Do you know what kings do?

Kings are the leaders. God made Jesus the head and highest King, and Jesus made you the king over the devil and his demons and over all the earth! Did you know that Jesus has given all of his kings a mission and a job to do on earth for Father?

Your work for God is to be His king and ambassador.

Do you know what an ambassador does? An ambassador is a person that is sent somewhere by their King to say and do what their King has told them. Your mission and job as king and ambassador is to believe Jesus and to show Father's love and kindness to all people. Raise your hand if you will accept the mission to be God's king and ambassador on earth.

Let's say, "YES, I AM A KING AND AMBASSADOR FOR JESUS!"

If you chose to be a king and ambassador for Jesus, you must learn how to use your super power of Holy Spirit to help you.

Put on your thinking cap. You need to think and practice doing things like Father and Jesus from now on. The first thing you must learn is how Holy Spirit will help you to show other people God's love and FORGIVE everyone.

If someone does something mean to you, should you hurt them back?

Let's think about what Jesus did. When Jesus was dying on the cross, what did he pray and say to his Father about the people?

Was he angry or mad at them?

No, Jesus prayed and asked his Father to forgive them. Jesus said that the people did not know what they were doing. Jesus showed love to everyone. He was not mad or angry that the people had listened to the lies of the devil.

Why do you think Jesus forgave everyone even when people hurt him and killed his body?

Jesus knows that when you do not forgive others, the devil makes hate and ugly things grow inside your heart. Father does not want that to happen to you.

Can you think of a person who did something bad or has been mean to you or to someone else?

What did Jesus tell you to do when someone is not nice to you?

Jesus said to forgive them, and to pray for them! Do you know why Jesus told you to pray for them?

Prayer is your secret weapon. Jesus knows that when a person does mean or unkind things they do not understand Father or His love. But when you forgive them, and pray for them, God can change their hearts. Do you know why Father and Jesus want their hearts to change?

Father and Jesus love everyone. They do not want anyone to be tricked by the devil. Do you remember what your secret weapon is?

Prayer is your secret weapon! When you pray and ask Father, Holy Spirit helps you, and Father will change their heart.

When you choose to be kind and show love to someone who acts mean, God said it is like pouring hot coals on top of their head.

Ouch! That would hurt! You may not see it happen right away, but watch and see how God's love ALWAYS wins!

Jesus has commanded you to forgive, but you have the choice if you will forgive someone or not. Did you know, Jesus said IF you do not forgive others that Father will NOT forgive you?

It's true! Sometimes you might have a hard time forgiving someone, but that is when you use your secret weapon and pray for them. Tell Father about it. Ask Him to help you, and God's power of Holy Spirit will help you to forgive.

Is there anyone you need to forgive?
If so, you can pray these words to forgive them now.

"Father,
Help me to forgive them!
Thank you Father. I forgive them now.
Will you change their and my heart to be kind and to know Your love?
Thank you Father! Amen."

This is your homework! Every morning, pray and talk to your Father. Tell your Father how much you love Him. Ask Him to help your heart to choose to be the first one to forgive and love others like He does in His Kingdom in heaven.

Remember, you are an ambassador and king for Jesus! So everywhere you go, you are a leader for Jesus to show others what God's kingdom looks like. Whenever someone asks, who is God's ambassador? You answer and say, "I am God's ambassador and king!"

Who is God's ambassador?
"I am God's ambassador and king!"
Amen!

The Purpose of the Foundation Curriculum

To firmly establish God's truth in each child's heart early in life so they will understand and know God's love and choose to live fully in the victory that Jesus Christ has already won.

The Goals

To show God's children his love, their true identity as children of God, their authority and power in Christ Jesus, their helper Holy Spirit, and how to pray to their Father in heaven.

FORGIVE

Story Book Lesson 4

The Objectives to understand from "Forgive" are:

1. You were Born-Again as a child of Father, in Christ Jesus.

2. You must learn how to do things like Father and Jesus, in love.

3. Father and Jesus forgave you.

4. Holy Spirit will help and guide you to choose right.

5. Holy Spirit is the spirit power of Father and Jesus in you.

6. Jesus made you a king and ambassador.

7. You are a leader on earth to show others God's Kingdom of love.

8. Father and Jesus want you to forgive others.

9. Your secret weapon is prayer to Father.

10. Holy Spirit will help you to forgive.

P.A.C.E.

Products and Activities
for Christian Education

For Free Follow-Up Activities to Reinforce This Story Book Lesson Please Visit
www.ABC-Jesus.com

Biblical quotes were from different versions of the holy Bible.

www.ingramcontent.com/pod-product-compliance
Lightning Source LLC
Chambersburg PA
CBHW041559040426
42447CB00002B/227